ART OF MIND

PHILOSOPOEMS TO THE WORLD

BY ORIGINAL CLYDE AIDOO

Copyright © 2011 Original Clyde Aidoo
All Rights Reserved.

ISBN: 0615429777
ISBN-13: 9780615429779

Library of Congress Control Number: 2010918622

CONTENTS

Use My Imagination P75

Philosopoem to the World

"Philosophy" is too limiting.
"Poems" are too restricting.

So I went and merged the two
&
This is my Philosopoem to You.

Come in, make yourself at home...
I could sure use the company
A lot more than the money.

Most my life I gagged at the "P" word.
They stunk like old cheese
&
I couldn't get the foul stench
offa me.
But I suppose you can call 'em "poems" if ya want...
Seems I'm "Mr. Poet" now so
There's no need to Front.
The truth is never too bold,
Can't measure greatness by copies sold,
Not in it for making a fortune,
Just need to make one less story untold.

Labyrinthine bookstores can be a real "Hike,"
Finding the right book can be a grind,
I've tried to read other poems,
Then I started "Envying the Blind."

My Mother always said, "Too Much of anything is bad,"
So I've always been cautious…
That's why when I read
One Line with a Dozen Metaphors:
It doesn't evoke emotion,
I only feel nauseous.

Within this composition
rests the spirit of poetry
&
The soul of a ballad,
With a Universal Recipe
prepared for any Palate.
In my words you'll never be lost,
They state the Facts of Life like Tootie,
I'll be sure to Hold Your Hand,
Tighter than Michael, Akon, & Hootie.

I figure I've made it this far,
So what's another hurdle?
I'm too unruly for Scholarly,
So Readers write their own Journals.

Too miserable to be cocky,
I'm only stating reality,
Critics only zero in on flaws,
That's called a Logical Fallacy.

Refuse me they may—
I might not get sponsored,
This book goes Harder than Porn
That's why this Shit is Uncensored…

Innovative lines/don't care for passé rhymes,
I got a "Sick Sense of Fashion"
that's why
Our Styles our Clashin'…

"80%" Gold,
100 % True,
If you like Real Themes
I wrote this book 4 you…

Can't promise to sell out
but
You won't regret Having Bought…
I can promise one thing:
These are all *My* thoughts.

Tired of the dull?
My plan will go without a hitch:
I'll shed a lil' light —
I'm here to "Flip the Switch."

If you're readin' dry,
This book will quench your thirst...
Though My name is Clyde:
Originality
Comes
First.

I plan to serve up critics
A slice of "Humble Pie,"
And by the time I'm through —
There'll be a
"Cause for Celebration..."

I'm a "Writer without a Cause"
Who always rocks "Headphones,"
I'm stuck in "Solitary,"
That's why I'm always alone.

Now everything in me has finally come out:
"Underneath,"
"Shell,"
"Veins,"
So come and
"Join the Club."

My Inspiration is to span Generations —
Spread Imaginations beyond all Limitations...

So cuddle on up, you may be one of the few:
This isn't just for me,
These are Philosopoems for You:

Ruffled Clouds Inc. Presents

An O.C.A. Experiment

In Association with RPRP Publications

Editing by

Clyde Aidoo
Bobo McGee

Special Consultants

Sonny Corinthos
Jason Morgan
Lucas Lorenzo Spencer
&
Emily Quartermaine (R.I.P) :0(

Artwork Provided by

Juliette Caron
Joe Cartwright
Daniel Colvin
Chet Davis
Judy Gilbert
Donna Marsh
John Penney
Lori Pratico
Kari Tirrell
Debi Watson

Executive Producers

Clyde Aidoo
Tony Stanza
Derek Meter

Art of Mind
Philosopoems to the World

By Original Clyde Aidoo

CHAPTER I

IT ONLY TAKES ONE TIME

(It Only Takes One Time)

A concealed hobby fermenting in dreams
Hours of labor—Turned to Months—
Even Years.
Hidden from Unseen Eyes —
Deemed pointless by the Unconscious —
"Cute" by friends and family.
Only destined to remain Unsent
Unviewed
Unaccredited/
Submitted
Published/
Accepted
Acclaimed:
It Only Takes One Time

Yearning
Loneliness
Subjected to tales of romance
&

The defeating of odds too great
to overcome oneself.
Pattern Rejection
Frustration
Hopelessness
Love:
It Only Takes One Time

Blackness
Entertaining
Pondering
Contemplating
So Unlike
Bluffing
Pleading
A part of the world today
Means a part of the world tomorrow...

It Only Takes One Time

In the Suburbs

<Set to the Melody of "In the Ghetto" by Elvis Presley>

On a cold and gray Chicago afternoon:
A middle class family decides to move
To the Suburbs...
...
Trying to find a home to fulfill their needs
But all they get instead is a bunch of trees
In the Suburbs...

So they send the youngest child off away to school
But the other kids don't take to a kid that's new
In the Suburbs...

Never thought to ask these other kids why
Maybe that's just the way of preppy Junior High
In the Suburbs...

Even though the boy never done one wrong
He spends all his time in his room alone
In the Suburbs...

The real world teens are really mean
So he finds fake friends on a ten-inch screen
In the Suburbs...

At his old home he would walk through town
Now eighty blocks long and not a single sound
In the Suburbs…

People don't you understand —
The kid needs a life instead…
Or he'll grow to be
A sad young man someday…
Take a look at you and me —
We have other people to see…
While this kid is stuck in the middle of a rut
Now the only life he sees is the neighbor's mutt…

In the Suburbs.
…
So he works to break free and gets his degree
Spends a few good years on a college spree…
He works to stay away…
He just needs to — get — paid…
And peace will begin to finally pierce through his mind…
…
Got a temporary job, but it didn't pay much
And now time's run out and he's out of luck…

Still dead set on the life he's never had…
He tries to find a job but the market's bad…
Now the only thing to show is a bunch of loans
After all that work he ends up right back home…

In the Suburbs.

...

And as his dreams die...

On a cold and gray Chicago afternoon:

Another middle class family decides to move...

To the Suburbs

Mr. Poet

I have always found
Your eloquent verse
And commanding tone
To be a ruse as Clever
And Skillful
As your cultured meters
and fitting rhymes.
For the cry I hear
Is not for help
or compassion —
Public sentiment and unbridled expression
lay on the surface of your page,
while between the lines translates ambition,
Insecurity,
A pursuit for validation as much as attention.
It is an effort worth a grand applause
And an admiring gleam...
For success is paid in generations
And failure is met with courtesy
And regard...
Just enough to get you through the next page.
I have accused your emotions of being
Artificial —
Masterfully Manipulated
to evoke the desired response.
Your delivery was lost in your genius lines
and cryptic stanzas:

Message Not Received

I resent you, your motives,

And Everything that you Stand For.

* * *

Perhaps as time passed
I may have been hasty,
And If I was wrong —
I apologize greatly.
Though our styles may differ,
And that will not change,
That is no excuse
To take motives in vain.
I now understand,
And I don't know why,
But my whole path changed:
Now I'm That Guy.

CHAPTER 2
FLIP THE SWITCH

Capacity Met

She's Mesmerizing both Inside and Out.
One look and you know she's special.
Something different in the very look on her face.
Every single characteristic unique.
She expresses herself in a way that pushes the human limits
of Intelligence and poise.
This could be made bearable
If her inimitable beauty was just from within.
One is reduced to stare shamelessly
From Afar,
While they take her until Capacity Met.
Her elegantly beatnik attire,
Her long dreadlocks bouncing freely upon her head —
Almost as gracefully as they dance in my eyes.
Her voice is a low, polished purr...
One less sense to have control of.
If only her effect was as gentle
As her nurturing presence &
Mocha-Cloaked Smile.

She's Mesmerizing both Inside and Out...

I Hate People Like That.

To Speak to a Sculpture

I Want to say you're a Goddess...
Not just in a physical or female sense...
I want to tell you to your face:
That you are an
Immaculate Human Being.
I want to tell this Sculpture
of its own meaning,
but despite my every perception,
You *are* just a Human Being.

If only you were a sculpture,
I could let my bare thoughts show...
But you are only a person,
One whom I barely know.
I see art imitating life,
That must be how you got your start...
For this is just a disguise,
But you are poorly playing the part.

Among the mirror of Your Museum,
I hope you'll stand beside me...
Then I could stare and finally speak
To the Sculpture that is before Us.

Flip the Switch

When I walked into your illuminating room,
My eyes correlated the Brightness.
It may have been this two-fold Ray,
That caused me to be so blind.
Rendered Dim,
I was unable to
look any further.
The room remained blissful
Still...
The only charge was
Ignorance.
When I dared walk
to the broader side,
I knew I might gain
Some Insight.
Though I was reluctant to see the light,
this was the only way
to shed some on You.
I decided to become your company,
even if risking
overstaying my welcome.

The room is undeniably bright,
for my eyes can only be so wrong,
But as your ray shined
down on others,
I found myself
In the Shade.

This light once as beaming
As the Heavens —
Now flickers like a
Domestic Watt,
After being upon
The cold, cold Shade,
I could now clearly see:
This room — while
Open for Others,
Was Closed Off to Me.

She may have set
The Conditions —
but I would leave on
My Own Terms:
I may not be the
Brightest Bulb,
but I too can shade
My Pitch...
Before I left the room,
I was sure to
Flip the Switch.

CHAPTER 3

THE LOSING BATTLE

The Losing Battle

When he showed me the mirror,
I saw he did a masterful job.
But as I left the shop,
I couldn't help wondering:
How many times
The clinic could resuscitate me.
When I returned to my room,
I found myself staring at
My own Reflection.
What I saw staring back at me
was an outright defiance of time.
I could see Da Kid holding on to the
Branch of Youth,
In spite of the winds of change.
In fact it was hard to fathom this display
of Resilience
Withering into a hoary stage.

But just as sure as I grew since birth,
And hair grew from my family jewels,
This image was to be as temporary
As my years in nursery school.

I saw heart, vibrancy and determination
To win this external struggle...
So at the end of this hanging stare,
I felt a heavy sadness:

For you may have won this fight,
Dear Friend,
But you're in a Losing Battle.

Prime's Death Bed

Death Awaits
This "Twenty-Something" year old chap.

I don't have much time left.
Few years at the most;
some months at the least.
My head aches at times, but
A tumor I don't have.
Never smoked much,
My lungs scan untouched.
Been known to throw a few back,
But my liver can still go
Another Round.
My Heart —
My Heart's Been Better...
But it keeps right on beating,
Even after taking a beating.

Not diagnosed with cancer,
Meningitis or Tuberculosis...
Have not contracted AIDS,
And for That I give Praise.
My Physicals are no thing,
My Blood-Work comes back clean,
The Doc says I'm in "top shape,"
No need to intervene.
My frame is ripped to the core,
I work out hardcore,
The weights go Rising Up...

While I'm Crashing to the floor.

It's a fall I will survive,
but I won't be the same again.

I'm lifting on borrowed time,
My life is on the line,
Grant this dying man One Wish —
before my Prime Reclines.

All the While

While you were making friends,
I was in my Den.
While you were having fun,
My work had just begun.
While you were on your dates,
I was working late.
While you were "tapping asses,"
I was mapping classics.
While you made a family,
I made a biography.

While you were in Love,
I chose to Write…
&
While I have your time:
I was wrong. You were Right.

Stranger of Tomorrow

this Thought you own
You really Borrow:
Never
Trust the Stranger
of Tomorrow.

Detention in the School of Life, Down Regret Hall, Room ZZZ-51

You've been very naughty...
Now Look, you're 51.
Go to your room for
Thirty More Years,
And think about
What You've Done.

CHAPTER 4

FATE'S BLUFF

Blessed

Lucky Ones
find a Dime on the Street,
and take it home
Without Pay.
They find great fame
in a well of
Empty Talent.
They are born into homes
of Privilege —
With Bills Paid
and Dreams Paved.
They fall into jobs of Nepotism,
While others fall further into Debt.
They welcome going out in
A Blaze of Glory,
but continue to evade death's bed...
They can ride life's wheel of fortune,
And never see black or red.

While they are drowning at the turn,
they are saved by a fleeting river.
Their skill is often at the bottom of the pile,
but they land at the top of the deck,
They play the numbers just like the rest,
yet only they hold the giant check.

To be fortunate is to be this lucky,
It's an envy that most possess...
But to flop on you
&
Win your love —
Is to be truly Blessed.

Poker Face

I've never been handed a Diamond,
No one ever gave me a Heart,
I'm left with Useless Clubs
In a life as black as Spades.
I am very weak,
My stack is always empty,
But I keep a stoic expression,
So no Tell will ever Trail Me.
Anybody can hold 2-7 —
And go all in with a Straight Face,
Just look at the cards *I'm* holding —
Then you'll see a Real Poker Face.
The cards you discard and muck,
are what I'd attribute to luck.
Any mug can mean
&
Wait to reel in Green
when you Know you'll get a Queen.
You only have to Pay,
Sit, Wait, and Fold 'Em...
I play without being dealt 'em —
That's why I'm good at Hold 'Em.
I'm still in with this Bad Hand,
Even without that Ace,
My life has given me practice,
I've mastered this Poker Face.

Fate's Bluff

They say good things come to those
Who Wait.
That Patience is a Virtue.
I've heard that great things happen
To those who expect least,
and that "Sooner or later,
Love is Gonna Getcha."
I've heard "You Can't Hurry Love,"
So I've just had to wait —
And Wait.
This would not cause alarm,
If my Emptiness had its own time zone...
If Professor Time could review leading circumstances,
And compassionately grant an extension.
The same sky that provides for some,
I've been waiting to provide for me,
My angel's name must be "Autumn,"
Cuz she sho'll ain't fallin'
to Me.
Tired of waiting I got up
&
Went Up,
Tried to find her with my
Head in the Clouds...
No matter which direction I look,
My search upholds to persist.

Ah, but I've heard and seen enough to know
Fate Will Jump In

When Ready...
I don't care what people say,
I know that help is on the way.

Others say "Beggars can't be Choosers..."
"Take what you can get,"
And let us not forget:
"Don't let time pass you by."
Why should I settle for leftovers —
With wounds from so many bites?
Or accept what I don't crave —
And ruin my appetite?
Mother fate will fill me up,
She's served so many others...
There is bound to be enough to go around:
We are all sitting
At the Same Table.

The last voice I hear is my own:
"Time is running out."
"Hurry the hell up!"
The last panicked voice insists,
"What are you waiting for!?"

Right as my head hits the wall,
I remember what I first heard:
How generous mother fate is.
No way will I go hungry,
even though
my ache continues to growl;
Surely this is just a test —

A game I'm willing to play.

Away with the middle men!
I speak to Fate myself — With a confident, daring smile:

"You Wouldn't leave me hanging,
Not when you've fed so many,
I'm only asking for one share,
It's not like I'm being greedy.
I know you'll get to me soon,
Just make it when you can,
Some say you are against me,
I know you are My Friend.
I won't listen to the voice
That says, "Enough is Enough,"
I'm on to this intricate game,
I think I'll call your bluff."

CHAPTER 5

VEINS

The Blade of Pride

I suppose I could make friends,
Many have tried to befriend me.
It feels like I'd be asking for help,
Even though it is They who approached Me.
I suppose I could ask friends and family
to pair me with a potential suitor...
But that would be like saying to them —
That I am a virtual loser.
It's funny how many do this,
and don't seem to think twice...
Still, it is the small things like these —
That would cut me like a knife.
So why would I rather be alone?
When this pain hurts even more?
While I attempt to answer that,
As you leave, Please shut the Door.

Veins

I will take a deep breath,
Then gladly cut myself...
And allow you to watch me bleed.
But you will not see my blade,
or even the blood oozing from the onset.
For every time you blink,
A new wound will appear...
Leaving you to wonder:
How long has he been bleeding?
And how have I not noticed before?

As you continue to wonder,
My invisible blade will cut deeper —
Through one vein after the next:

Beginning with the superficial veins...
Though these cuts may seem petty,
These cuts often bleed the most,
As much as any artery.
I'll proceed to the Deep Veins,
Which will really make you squirm —
This exposes my essential core,
The more you flit, the more I yearn.
I need these veins I'm cutting,
For without them I have no heart...
To flee while I still bleed,
Means you too would have no heart.
This blood count cannot be replenished
By even the mightiest of valves,

It is my will that leaves me standing,
Though even J. Andrews cannot say how.
These veins I will continue to cut,
Leaving them open for the world to see,
Though Some veins I will not cut,
They will always stay with me.
Long after my body runs dry,
And I am left to rot,
The coroner can dig for days,
Some parts cannot be sought.
When my body belongs to the world,
With nothing left to save,
After all my carving and cleaving,
Some veins I'll take to the grave.

Underneath

You know, it ain't easy standing here naked,
So please find something good to say...
I know you didn't want to see people naked,
but please find something good to say.
This wacky act of liberation
is really
Courageous Underneath...
I know, right now the last word
that comes to your mind is
"underneath."
Though I know I'm showing too much,
Would it kill you to give a compliment?
My being crazy enough to be nude
shouldn't discredit an honest compliment.
My body is really quite nice —
I often work out...
Look at my chest, pecs and biceps...
Can't you tell that I work out?
My abs are pretty tight,
And I know my package is good...
It is, though, isn't it?
Please tell me my package is good.
If it's not, go back to my biceps,
My chest, or my abs.
Which one do you like most?
My biceps, my chest, or my abs?
No, don't call me those names —

That should not discredit my body...
Ok, fine, you can call me names,
Just as long as you credit my body.
Just Please give me a compliment!
Any compliment will do!
Those like me are standing here naked,
Hell, it's the least that you can do.

CHAPTER 6

THE STRENGTH OF A MAN

Shell

The reason I'm in this Shell
Is because
I'm a shell of what I used to be...
Once out in front of the world,
Now trapped inside of me.
I miss being free,
Loose,
A Jester Among Men...
Now the only time I come out —
Is when I let you in.

Shut Out from the Inside — Not the Outside

My palms are sweaty,
There's a frog in my throat,
That may be the reason
It feels like I'm gonna croak.
My speech may stutter,
Pause, Stammer & Slur…
I know it's because of me,
She thinks it's because of her.
My anxiety doesn't discriminate
Against gender and sex…
It isn't beauty and breasts,
It's the sight of human flesh.
Either hairy or buxom
could make my chest pave,
I didn't always live this way…
Only since
I've dwelled in this cave.

So Close Yet So Far

Ooooh I can feel your energy,
Just as real as if your skin,
I can taste you right in front of me:
Intoxicating as Seagram's Gin.
It's clear you're very pretty,
But you're not "too good" for me.
We may never be here again,
And you feel more familiar than kin.
Yet whenever this happens it seems
That something always stands in-between…

How can something so Grand —
Be thwarted by Circumstance?
We defied all laws of motion —
To meet here in this moment.
We've met from a journey so far —
Just to settle for remaining afar…
How can we be So Close —
And yet stay so Very Far?

The Strength of a Man

We are supposed to have
Strength.
The strength to steal hearts
Right from the Owner's Chest.
The Strength to evoke
The Power of Love.
The strength to
Build roads, towers, and
Scaffolds...
The strength to leave
The elderly, and our women and children
Baffled.
We are supposed to have the
Strength
To mold, shape and create...
The strength to make and provide,
and keep our families safe.

I am just A Man.

If I could be more strong —
I'd build a life for us,
It wouldn't even take long —
I just need these roadblocks gone.

If I had the strength
to clear all They put in our way,

And leave just me and you,
I wouldn't have to say:

I am just A Man.

Yes, You Should Be Nervous

If I said you
Shouldn't be Nervous,
Well then I would be lying...
This isn't a perfect world,
You don't get credit for trying.
Don't you know what's at stake?
Companionship, love, even kids...
Some say you shouldn't worry...
Ha! Who are they trying to kid?
That Speech
That Game
That Girl —
All have different consequences,
And If you don't perform well:
The withdrawal will be relentless.
So hey, man, stiffen up!
Don't look so darn comfortable!
You might end up in a hooptie,
When you could've had a convertible.

When You Can't Muster Up the Courage

Even though you may be afraid,
Only you know your little secret...
Even though you may be a Coward:

It just takes
The Guts
to pretend
You
Have Guts.

CHAPTER 7

DISAPPOINTMENT'S WAITING ROOM

6/23: 25 Hundred

Your clock may hold
My final fate,
But I will control
Today's Date.
Your log may change
for Mindless Sheep,
My date will change
when Sleep's Complete.

Keep It in the Dark

You don't hear any whimpering
from me,
So this emission is not me
"Crying..."
It must be ocular strain,
Not the grease of my
Soul Frying.

I Woke Up In a Bed of Clichés

I woke up in a bed of clichés,
In this bed I remain to lay.

Crying is too unlike me,
A dry tear this cannot be...
I'm certain I wasn't sobbing,
So I didn't cry myself to sleep.

Laziness is more my forte,
This must be chronic fatigue...
I Know I have a Reason to Get Up,
Yet in this bed —
Still — I Lay.

Disappointment's Waiting Room

I'm sure you'll disappoint me
when you can,
I'll patiently wait my turn...
It's my fault for thinking you're different,
When you're just another way to burn.
I'm sure there are many others,
So yes, I'll gladly wait...
I know it could be a while....
This world is an awful big place.

You count
7 Billion People,
I see
7 Billion Disappointments:
While others are out on Dates,
I'm busy making Appointments.

Holiday Spirit

It's the 4th of July and
The Bombs are Bursting in Air.
Eyes turn toward the sky,
And today there's a fire
In Everyone's eyes.
It's a celebration of Independence
&
A Liberation of Life.
Sparklers and Grills blaring to the rhythm
of Blaring tunes,
Kids soaked and stoked
&
Couples
Streaming and Screaming.
Air's transparent hue
is Painted
Red, White and Blue!

Freedom sings in an anthem for U—A!
They, Them, You…
Not Us.

For Me…

For me it's just Another Day.

Without someone to share,
There is no reason to care.

This day is as dull as yesterday,
And just as bleak as tomorrow…
It was the same with the last event,
as it will be with the one to follow.

Holidays are a National Declaration —
Transmitted for the world to hear it…
Yet I cannot Boost Life —
Because I Have No Spirit.

CHAPTER 8

SMALL TALK

The Extent of my social contribution to a stranger, new acquaintance, or my closest friend on this dark and dreary ordinary day/My strongest approach to the most desirable scent coated flesh in the room or the secret admiration of the past 18 months of whom I have never spoken/My sentiments to a shipwrecked long lost relative whose kinship I hold near and dear to my heart

Hey.

How's it goin'

Hell-O

God, not this again...
Ok, here we go, "Hey!"
This greeting could not
be avoided:
You were directly
Along my Way.
I can't take much more of this...
When will this
Vicious Cycle be Broken?
Day after weathering Day:
I Greet
Whom I've Barely Spoken.

Waving to a Professor

You pick up my every error.
You are a blood hound for English Gramar.
You can sniff out the smallest mistake...

You remember my every absence,
Without reviewing my marks...
You sit there without ever flinching,
More stubborn than Rosa Parks.
You could snatch a blowing whisper,
Your alertness doesn't cease to amaze...
Which is why I find myself wondering:
How could you *not* have seen my wave?

Small Talk

Let's talk about Sports.
My vicarious life
is much more inspiring.
Bring up the weather —
Chatter about rudimentary meteorology
conceals my dark clouds.
We can talk about the news...
Stories of troubles from worlds away
Arouse more empathy and concern
than what is staring right at you.
We can even discuss the job market...
And stand on equal ground
in our grievance against oppression.
But do not masquerade small talk
as a heart to heart with a stranger,
or an acquaintance
I don't care to know.

This warning is probably best dispatched
to the family friends and relatives
who merely wish to catch up:
I understand it isn't intentional,
Which is why I'm making this crystal:
Do not Ask me about my Day —
It hurts to say what you want me to say.
And do not ask about my status,
As it is not what I want it to say.

SMALL TALK

I'm sure to you this is small talk,
And to hurt is not your goal,
But what you consider mere small talk —
Is a violation of my soul.

CHAPTER 9

THE HIKE

The Rain before the Storm

You think that This is darkness?
You think that This is sad?
You think you've seen my worst?
You haven't seen the half.

You Think this is me crying,
You Think you've seen my tears...
You think that This is bad?
Get at me in ten years.

Forecast: Cloudy with Inpouring but No Signs of Rain

I speak of tears
that have never
Seen Daylight,
My eyes may be strained,
But no mist clouds my sight.
My hue may represent
the optical Dark Cloud,
But if I should pour —
It won't be out loud.

Before the Blizzard Starts

It's a warm one today.
Hurry up and Join Me...
It may be nice for now,
But soon it will get chilly.

I can see it in your eyes,
You could feel the same...
Time is running out,
Before this fire wanes.

I know that I could love you
With all the warmth
that's in my heart...
You just have to love me back —
Before the Blizzard Starts.

Feel my heart beat now,
Before the wind blows in...
Because once you've felt my chill —
You'll never feel again.

The Hike

At sunrise, as the sky begins to clear:
So begins The Hike.

With nothing new on the horizon,
I still aim to make the outdoors great.

I'll settle for making it back intact.

On weekends I may roam unconstrained,
On This day I lug a Backpack —
Intended to forefend fail,
but Useless
on This rigorous trail.

Bitter winds, whipping debris, and stony ground
Renders my body achin',
True pioneers must stay the course,
And keep walking the path less taken.

My algid chill cannot repress
The labored sweat that drops
as briskly as the sloping temperatures.
Still, I march uphill with poise and tenacious proficiency.
Every step commands determination,
As the earth stiffens and
the Cold winds
Continue to pick up Pressure.

THE HIKE

As I stand in place,
Yet blowing against the wind —
I eye the formidable
Mountain.

I Harness.
And I Climb.

In the face of conditions
that would make the ordinary man
fall off the steep end,
or camp out,
I choose to climb.

Amidst any Storm,
Beneath any dark hovering cloud,
You will Never see any rain on this face.
Only a hardened brow
and staid visage.
Amidst the most severe
Climates,
Among the Highest of Mountains,
I smile tirelessly,
and laugh incessantly.

I have seen the bottom,
I have felt the hardest drop...
I may fall by nightfall,
but right now — I'm at the top.

CHAPTER 10

JOIN THE CLUB

The Complaint

You oughtta quit this day job,
You are a Master of Illusion...
What I Knew was mutual admiration
Has warped into total confusion.
I thought that smile was special,
Meant only to me from you...
Now I come to find out —
It's literally for All who come through.
I guess that makes me the mark;
Damn, I was a real dope...
I let myself build up hope,
Just to watch it go up in smoke.
Yes, you need to quit this day job,
You'd do better turning tricks —
Oops, I meant doing tricks...
Well, However you get your kicks.
On second thought you oughtta keep it,
Your magic is probably through...
It's only a matter of time
before the others see right through you.

The Warning

I get it.
You are agreeable beyond all reason.
You laugh at all our jokes,
And look soulfully into our eyes.
You connect individually to us all,
As we all connect individually to you.
Your angelic glow is brighter than any halo,
One glimpse is all it takes,
and the rest we are dying to know.

Your beauty is more than Enough,
No need to work this game
So eloquently...
Oh, nice girl, please let me be...
or
I'll be forced to take you seriously.

Join the Club

I've Heard that laugh before...
Now I hear it going in his ears.
I've seen that look before,
I'd hoped that sight was
for my eyes only.
I was bound to make my move,
Now I feel I need to move.
I thought I'd have my way,
Now I think I'm in the way.
My screened interrogation
Turns up a statement of,
"Just Friends..."
I wonder if that's Your call,
or if you're awaiting a call
From Him.
Your sense of comfort with him —
I find it hard to ignore...
Just when I thought it was just him,
I turn to find eight more.
I search for any detectable gap
That shows the space between
Me and Him...
And him and him and him...
And him and him and him...
And him....

And him....

The difference may very well be:

I want what they could've taken...
You say he's "just a friend,"
I wonder if that's because
He's Taken.
Your friendship
Seems Disposable:
You both
mingle and associate a lot...
I cannot relate —
Our time is all I've got.
I won't be made a fool,
Reading too much in what they
Skim Through...
They have "lady friends,"
While All I want is You.
The next time we work together,
Let's try & work together...
To shift past our same-clad peers...
And begin a private endeavor.

CHAPTER 11

THE GREAT DIVERSION

80 %

The kid is strange.
Of this he makes No secret,
We all can relate,
Only he can't keep it.
Perhaps he doesn't want to,
Perhaps he doesn't care,
Perhaps he lives the truth,
While we wouldn't dare.
His offbeat ain't fad,
No Goth or Glam,
Wasn't punked
Into Emo,
No regnant Sham.
Enthused about shticks
Reserved for misfits,
Alone without cliques,
Couldn't change for shit.
His strange is in his speech,
His shape and his feet,

He walks his own way,
And marches his own beat.
Him we wouldn't wannabe,
For his strange we can see,
Not quite the same —
As the strange in you and me:

: She bleeds on blades
: She fucks for grades
: He masturbates
Eight times a Day.
: She makes men learn
Of female scorned,
One tiny trip —
All assets Burned.
: He'll inhale Craig
for a nom'nal fee,
Then pay to see
Bestiality.
: He smells strange drawers
to sniff and see
if his butt-budd
smells just like he.
: She eats her meal
Then throws it out,
not in the trash,
but out her mouth.
Her glass says fat,
But it's not true,
In actual fact,
She's a size 2.

: She's simply corked
as a-foul-bat,
: And he's a dork
Who cages rats.
: He presses down
when he is done,
but he neglects
to wipe his bum.
: She pledges love,
Her stance is set,
Three weeks ago
They had just met.
: She lends her ear,
A friend indeed,
Then puts it out
On her newsfeed.

All that you see's
What they Present,
But they're akin
to Harvey Dent.

* * *

His strangeness is not only found
at the surface —
It is Aboveboard.
To relate is to confess
That it's a trait we All possess —
Manifested in forms
as piddling as mannerisms

to the bizarre and
absurd.
My fellow self-aware accusers of the world
often hide
Just as cunningly
Behind the very same crowd
Of trait-less faces.
We misuse "All"
To justify us all.
In reality,
Some numbers are
as the calculator reads.

Yes some add up to
What-they-Present,
They roughly fit
20 %

Mute Point

Everybody's talking about it,
Haven't you heard?
It's the Hottest Topic
from Omaha to Pittsburg.
Figures on the tube,
In-crowds in the loop,
It seems like anybody in sight
Has a Point of View.
The consensus has been rendered
but that one guy was astute…
His voice will be drowned out —
The Best Points are Turned Mute.

The Great Diversion

An Author writes his novel —
Hoping he'll make it big...
A Musician plays in his Band —
Hoping for a Larger gig.
An Artist paints a canvas —
Hoping to be on display...
Broadcast Majors plan to Announce —
They study Play by Play.
An Athlete Runs Many Miles
To be on
A Walk of Fame...
A Poet develops Verse —
Desperately
Throwing Out
Her Name.
Well-Connected Dreamy Eyes
Think they can save TV,
One Network after another —
They're brought back to Reality.

Others just want to get by;
They live just for the payout...
Right when there's time for Love —
They're right back on their Way Out.

A Mechanic Repairs
A Therapist Cares
An Accountant Counts
While Salesmen Discount

THE GREAT DIVERSION

Carpenters Construct
Businessmen Conduct
Fashionistas Design
Architects Align
A Butcher Chops
A Janitor Mops
A Valet Parks
A Detective Narks
A Cabby Drives
A Sailor Dives
Acupuncturists Puncture
Engineers Structure
A Chef Fries
A Pilot Flies
An Agent Spies
A Politician Lies
And Workers Work
And Workers Work
And Work and Work...

They Work and Work and Work,
They Dream, They Sweat, They Chatter,
It's all a Great Diversion
From the One thing that Really Matters.

The Funniest Joke Never Told

It Was the Funniest Joke Ever Uttered...

It wasn't on a TV Screen...
Not on an elevated stage...
There were no hosted seats,
No airway to be played.
The guy was pure genius,
The delivery was sharp and quick,
The funniest part was the content —
Though only his targets were meant to Get It.
It was drop dead hilarious.
I wish you could have
Heard It.
I wish *I* could have heard it —
Said it...

It Was the Funniest Joke Ever Told.
Only two others heard it...
But they were too busy engaging each other —
To even bother to notice.

The second funniest joke ever told
Was in an intimate clique,
They called it a "Private Party,"
We've all been to one like it.
One joke was the funniest of all —
It stayed between those walls —
It was forgotten by sunrise —
Meant only for nightfall.

THE GREAT DIVERSION

The third funniest joke ever told
Was at the family table,
The punch line was full of love —
A lot of us wouldn't get it.
'Twas one rambunctious time,
With the youngest's silliest line,
The table Always has laughter,
But none quite like this time.

The fourth funniest joke ever told
Was between a happy couple,
Up long on the phone,
His jokes continued to double.
One was the funniest of all,
It was the funniest
He ever said,
The line must have eavesdropped...
Soon after it had dropped dead.

Def Jam, Circa '93 —
Had the fifth funniest ever told,
Now That One was televised,
But I forgot the episode.

CHAPTER 12

SICK SENSE OF FASHION

Use My Imagination

You looked a lot better
before I saw All of you...
Please continue this fantasy,
I can wait to come to.

You sounded much better —
Before I heard all your tracks,
Some songs are better unheard,
I wish you had took That One back.

Time stood still,
Frozen in a daze,
But I bolted on out
When you told me your age.

Superstar you Are,
I admire your Charm,
The tabloids don't hurt You,
It's My Image they Harm.

No, no — Don't tell me your past,
I don't want this Perception
To be My Last.

Some people always ask:
"How did they do that?"
I just applaud the Magic,
And skip the chat.

My vision of you
Is Larger than Life,
Don't bring me back down
from this Cloudy Height.

The Imagination can roam free of All Boundaries...
All it Takes:
Is just a Few Limits.

No, Baby, Leave it ON!

No, really, I didn't mean it…
I just wish you didn't take off
Your Make-up.
I swear, you don't look like Hamma-Time…
So now can we Please make up?

Sick Sense of Fashion

Alright, Very Funny...
Yes — it was a good one,
Yes, indeed.
You have a
Sick Sense of Fashion,
And Now the Joke's on me.
What happened to the girl from last night?
Did she leave the earth
as you left the club?
Today you're a female Clark Kent,
Superwoman flew up above.
They say that change is good,
I only wish that you'd change back...
But why would you do that?
And ruin your little laugh.
I thought I liked your booty,
I thought I liked your breasts,
I thought I loved your body,
All-Along I loved your dress.

CHAPTER 13

FALSE ADVERTISING

False Advertising

She has all the makings
of a Summer Clearance...

You'd swear that she is cheap
As the talk that trails her feet.
She makes the haute couture
Look as dowdy as hand-me-downs.
She can take a dress by Prada
and make it seem
Like she's wearing Nada.
Some may call her dress too tight,
But we'd say it don't fit
Just Right.
How can she not be open?
When her goods are right on display?
She may fool some novice consumers —
But I see this day by day.
While she may seem to be a tag sale,
Tell me why these window-shoppers?

Her fruit is forbidden for a reason:
She only allows handpicked sharecroppers.
So while others have funds denied,
I don't bother to try…
For her sign may say, "For Sale,"
But I Know her Price is too High.

Not So Fast

She looks Real Loose, seems
An Easy Hammer —
Ought'a Do Her.
She wants an Alpha,
Really
Superman
Can Only Screw Her.

All She Wants to Do is Grind

<Set to the Melody of "All She Wants to Do is Dance" by Don Henley>

<Saxophone Intro>

...

I can tell by the way she looks at me —
The Lust is in her Eyes...
But All She Wants to Do Is
Grind-Grind |
Yes it's written all Over Her,
I'm gettin' between dem thighs...
But all she wants to do
Is Grind... |
Ain't no doubt about it,
I can see it in her moves...
Yet all she wants to do is
Grind-Grind |
The time for lookin' is over,
I'm 'bout to make my move...
But all she wants to do is Grind... |

I press my body into hers,
Rubbin' on her behind...
By this time tomorrow,
I know that Ass is mine/
If she wanted to raise this bar...
She got a rise out of me...

FALSE ADVERTISING

She needs to skip the foreplay,
And hand over them keys —

But all she wants to do is Grind...

Been thrustin' for over an hour now,
So Hard I can barely stand,
I can tell she's as hot as I am,
Just by where she placed my hand/
My fingers are free to roam now...
This chick could never say "no..."
But all she wants to do is Grind... |

At this point of the night,
We're on our 15th song...
The bar will soon be closing,
Oh I know it won't be long...
Till we're arranging our own sheets,
And banging to our Own beat...

But All She Wants to Do Is —

All She Wants to *Do* is Grind...

No Hittin' from Behind...

<Saxophone Intermission>

...

She likes to Partaay

WHOOOOOOO

But she won't Get Down

NOOOOOOOO

Cuz All She Wants Do Is Grind...

...

It's only a matter of time —
Before I'm in her bed...
We've been grindin' so damn hard now,
I ain't sure which is my big head/
Just when I least expect it,
She moves on to another guy...
You've got to be fuckin' kidding me,
This is just a big joke, right?
She dances with that whole group now —
God-Damnit that girl was mine...

But All She Wants to Do Is —

All She Wants to *Do* is Grind...

And it Happens all the Time...

<Close Out>

CHAPTER 14

PROMISCUOUS BIRTH

Promiscuous Birth

Only on this
Flawed Earth:
The more people you love,
The more people breed hate.

PROMISCUOUS BIRTH

Rita Faltoyano

Her Beauty was Nobility.
Her Form was Poetry.
Her Motion was a Symphony.
She didn't just "act sexy,"
She acted it out.
She didn't just take the money,
She put it in her mouth.

Her features and appeal
Topped the finest in our Time...
Yet Maxim couldn't list her,
&
Magazines couldn't Cover her.

She wasn't a comely athlete,
or a famed Hollywood Actress...
Her gap from your
"Common Whore,"
Is that she paid her taxes.
Not worthy of being acclaimed,
Because she sucked on screen,
All it takes is one shot,
And you will see a Queen.
She's no Jenna Jameson,
Who hit the X Lottery,
She's just another slut —
Who lacks any dignity.

Yet her mien and natural majesty

Was the very portrayal of Royalty.

She doesn't need recognition,
Or your biased lists...
It wasn't Berry or Alba
who was the sexiest to exist.

Her difference between the stars
And Goddesses not on TV:
She doesn't just look the part,
She allows the World to see.

Being the Very Best —
Means Submitting Evidence.
Of all the models of Youth —
Only They submit the proof.

The media has control
of names the world ought'a know...
But I will never forget:
Rita Faltoyano.

An artist can have the luster
of any Star Ever Born...
The world will not prompt credits:
It's only filthy porn.

Rainbow Bride

Most Grooms would Love
A
Bride in White...
But most cannot
Give that Gift.
So Grooms settle for a few botches
And red left-breast stains.
It no longer matters.
A new beginning calls for
White...Right?
I know I certainly would love a bride
Worthy of White...
Not just physically but spiritually...
but I guess physically is all we can really ask for...
But how many really
Get that Gift?
So...since that gift is so far out of reach...
And there will be color regardless...
Well,
Then...
I see nothing wrong with choosing a Rainbow —
Even if They color her a "Ho."

You can't try to bleach colors,
It just won't come out right...
You can rearrange and try to match...
But it just won't come out white.
2 shades darker or 200...
White just isn't White...

Sometimes light colors try to pass as white,
or think they are close enough...
But white just isn't white:
Close just isn't enough.
Instead of picking a light,
A grey or a pink shade...
He went and got a Rainbow —
I still say he's got it made — although They think
otherwise.

And even if they don't last or workout...
Sometimes even white doesn't come out the other end
The way you thought it would.

I said, "He's a lucky guy..."
They say, "She's a Ho, not a Housewife..."
He'll have Great Sex for a
Long, Long Time:
The next best thing to a Bride in White.

CHAPTER 15

WALLS

(No Subject)

If only there were some
Magical Box,
Sent straight from the Gods above,
Where I could search worldwide —
I'm sure I'd find my love!
With the infinite possibilities and faces,
The World would have no more
Lonely People!

Oh, Boy! That would be just perfect!
It'd be too easy to find Miss Right!
(As I would soon find out....
"Too Easy" was exactly right....)

Perfect Strangers

So let me get this straight...
I want to make sure I understand:
I'm a stranger cuz we never met...
And he's Not cuz he's in a band?
It's clear we have much in common,
Our profiles are a Perfect Match...
I may not be a Big Fish,
But I'm still a damn good catch!
Why are you so eager to meet him?
When he doesn't care if you're alive?
And if you think he does,
You're only telling yourself a lie.
If you really want to meet him,
You'll have to get in line...
You deleted what could've been real,
Just because we met online.

Walls

Pick up the electric hammer,
Let's break down this
Massive Wall...
It won't take much strength,
All you have to do is Call.

Don't just write on my wall,
We can destroy this
Mighty Wall...
I swear it won't take much strength,
Just one, single Call.

Thank you, I got your message...
Now we're on the right track...
I reply, we don't message again —
That makes two steps back.

Some Abstract Walls are just Artificial,
Others —
Moreover Superficial...
These walls that are keeping us apart —
Are the Real Issue.

Past Generations plowed through walls
without obstruction.
Pens, Planes, Memories, Trains...
Would lead old friends back together.
Some drove through states —
Or flew through gates —

Just to see that familiar face...
Now the only thing between
Old friends —
Is a link on MySpace.

If we could reunite in person,
I could watch your countenance rise...
There lays my profile pic —
Which ruins the big surprise.
New friends the saddest make me,
When we met we had a ball...
The next day we had these walls,
No more motivation to Call.

These walls cause a sickness:
They make All friends lethargic —
To fight this epidemic:

You mustn't live between them.

Stop writing on these walls,
That message meant nothing
At all,
Let's mallet past our walls,
Only one of us has to Call.

CHAPTER 16

THE OTHER 1S

The Other 1s

Don't look at me like I'm a freak
With a damaged chromosome,
Yes I am alone,
But I am not alone.

Next time you assume I'm a Breed
of
A Kind that's just begun...
Remember these words I tell you:
I'm not the Only 1.

A Friend in Need

I may never reach out,
That doesn't mean
I wouldn't pull *you* out.
If you need a friend and peer,
Just know Da Champ is Here.
From those of my Blood
to the most Feculent Beggar:
My companionship is free of charge.
Any Strengths or Attributes you Lack,
I'll apprize your Face —
Not crimson your Back.
This isn't an empty verse,
The phrase is true, but in reverse:
If you are a man in need,
I'll be a friend indeed.

Waterfalls

Let the Water fall.
I will be here
To catch you...
I don't care if I get wet,
Let me be your tissue.
You can take it to the banks:
One day my river may flow,
And you'll be the first to know.
We can catch our Waterfalls,
No pair of arms are ever too small.

Saturday Night Live

If I could take one thing from
SNL,
And apply it to my own life,
You could capture my thought as it happens,
I wouldn't have to Think Twice.
It wouldn't be the jokes and laughter,
Or standing the test of time,
It'd be that final minute —
When the night's work comes to a wind.
Each Saturday,
I'd thank my friends for coming out
while standing with my trusted gang,
And even when the fun is over,
We'd still chum around and hang.
I'd apply that same communal mirth,
As my band continues to play —
Those very same homely tunes,
as our souls continue to sway.
The entire show makes me laugh,
I smile cheek to cheek…
The best part of it all —
We'd do it all again Next Week.

The SIU Buddy Anthem

<Set to the Melody of the "Good Times" Closing Credits>

<Piano Intro Plays for 4 seconds>

MMMMMMM-mmhmmmmm...

Just lookin' out of the windowww...
Watching the girls pass byyyy...

Wondering why this school is full of guys —

GOOD TIMES!

YAYEYEAHHHH

GOOD TIMES!

Hangin' with friends on the weekends!
Getting a dance when you can!

Festivals of Sausage!

Good Times!

Easy lay cockblocks...

Good Times!

Never-Ending Boyfriends!

Good Times!

Frats with all the Hoodrats!

Good Tiiiiiimmmeess

Ain't we lucky we got 'em...

<Closing Piano>

GOOD TIMES!!!!!!!!!!!!!!!!!!!!!!

CHAPTER 17

BACK UP

Too Spontaneous, Too Late

It's a little too late
to Go out of My Way,
&
In case you didn't notice —
A Little Notice
Goes a Long Way.

Back Up

My plan was to be with you,
Till I discovered that
I was your Plan B...
I told you to see your way out,
And yet you keep
Calling up for the D.

Rearview

So here it ends, my friend,
Until we meet again.
I may be in Your rearview,
But I will never forget you.
You can erase my number,
But you can't erase the past —
No matter how Far Gone.

I Want You to be Happy

I know everybody says this —
But I really Do want you to be happy.
I figure we can only
End up with one anyway...
So why should the others
Have to pay?
It didn't work out between us,
But I'll meet her,
And you'll meet him.
So what's the sense in wishing ill-will,
When we both will get our fill?
And even if I am false —
Even if only I don't find someone...
That makes these words even truer.

I wouldn't wish this on Anyone.

CHAPTER 18

UNDERGROUND RAILROAD

Soul Food

Cornbread and Collard Greens
Is one thing,
You may even refuse golden beans,
But answer me just one thing:
Who doesn't like a chicken wing?

No tongue can renounce
Fried Chicken,
Regardless of region or pigment,
To push this off on one group —
Is imagination's own vivid figment.

Pig feet can surely be beat,
Chitlins may take their toll,
But to not like ribs or chicken —
Is to exist without a soul.

Acting Black

Some say that I act white,
Even though I'm clearly black...
If I held a gun to your head,
Then would you take it back?

Un-Emancipated

Gosh Darn, I really wanted To Express Myself
In my Own Words
and voice key trackin'...
Black Man you can't do that,
I guess white folks ho'd da Patent.

180 Discrimination

What do you call a man
Who doesn't walk and talk
The Same?
Well some may call him a Goofy,
Others will say he's a Lame.

While others walk on free,
We place ourselves in the hot seat...
Now it's Our strangers we can't look in the eye
Without hanging from a tree.

Instead of embracing our differences,
You look for any faults...
Instead of acquitting our people,
Your judgment won't let them walk.

Underground Railroad

They seem to walk
The Path of Righteousness —
Of the "decent" and the "plain…"
Others are Clearly Ran —
But they're All aboard the train.

The kids around the block,
Have been around the block.
The teens behind the tracks,
Have earned their share of tracks.
Adults maintain innocence —
While Dipping in pleasures of sin,
Their partners would find them guilty…
But they're busy expanding the trend.
It's a Nationwide Movement!
Harriet Tubman would be proud!
The naïve have no idea —
Of what happens Underground.
If you wish to climb aboard,
A ticket you'll surely find,
but do not wait too late —
Or you'll get left behind.

Black & White

African-American
Korean
Mexican
Pacific Islander
Caucasian
Chinese
Puerto Rican
Native Americans
Japanese
Dominican
Afro-Mexican
Afro-Puerto Rican
Afro-Dominicans
Arab Americans
Asian-Puerto Rican
Chinese-Dominican
Chinese-Mexican
Afro-Korean
French-Italian
Italian
Japanese-French
Irish-Puerto Rican
Irish-Mexican
Irish-Thai
Thai
Cuban
French Cuban

Afro-Cuban
Cuban-Dominican
Filipino
Filipino-Thai
Afro-Japanese-Cuban-French-Thai
Caucasian-Mexican-Italian
Mulatto
Afro-Caucasian
Caucasian-Mexican-Italian
Portuguese-American
Red-Bone
Argentinean
Mexican-Arab-Native American-Polish-Irish-German-Spanish-Japanese-Filipino...
Spanish
...

Incredible that out of all these
Races and Ethnicities:
There's not a single touch of gray.

Characters you'd assume could vary,
With so many diverse nationalities...
Though apparently in these
United States:
There's only
Two Personalities.

Dazed and Confused

I smiled as I went
out the door,
and laughed as I walked
To the Bus,
If I were only 12 shades lighter,
You'd notice a constant Blush.
Today I find odd humor —
In what all others pass...
Tonight I still have laughter —
Not nearly out of gas.
I may be cracking up,
And thus I'm cracking up —
For I know I felt pain in my brain,
My misery was plain,
If this is how it feels to go mad —
Then who would want to be sane?

To what do I owe this new found joy?
Did my drive begin to kick in?
This feeling is from Parts Unknown —
To the typical State I'm in.
Today, I find myself playing
When I often sit out of the world's
Black & White Deals...
I'd like to credit myself —
But I owe it to these
Blue & White Pills.

CHAPTER 19

"EXPRESSION" THE ORPHAN

Ultimate Law

Enter Artist
V for Vendetta
Obsessed with Greatness
Love Can Wait
Ultimate Law
Tatted on the Back
I was a Boy
On I Prevailed
Now a Man

The Kid's Got Soul

Don't got many possessions.
Don't have my own lease…
Despite my creative obsessions,
My dreams drift & decrease.
My body has hit the mat —
More times than I care to count…
But my heart refuses to let me —
Stay down for the full ten-count.
In spite of my streak of losses,
One thing is on a roll,
Still after all these years —
The Man's Got Soul.

To the Woman I Love

Today is Saturday,
&
I'm still trying to decide what to do...
Between:
Women,
Parties,
Nightclubs,
Bars,
Games,
Casinos,
And
Booze...
It's a no contest,
This one was easy to choose.
Out of all the things in the world
That I could choose to do...
I'll Grocery Shop with You —
On Saturday Afternoon.

Dynasty

We had a good run.
Though it had
Its Ups and Downs...
Sometimes more down than up,
But sometimes the best love is tough.
We've teamed together too long,
Leave now I wish I could...
I know you don't want me to feel bad,
But Change would do me Good.
We've been a hell of a Dynasty,
but
It never ending would be a travesty.
I want to branch out now,
I just couldn't figure out how.
I may never have cleaned our home,
But together we sure cleaned house...
The only one you should commit to for this long —
Is your Beautiful Spouse.
Our Dynasty has spanned two decades,
Yet Still we await our rings...
Though we've won over every battle,
I hope to move on to Bigger Things.

"Expression" the Orphan

You don't control what I do,
And this isn't
"Giving you Lip..."
Just because we're Kin,
Doesn't Mean
We're Joined
At the Hip.
I may still roost in the nest,
But my mind is free to Wander.
You can take back the key,
But you can't lock creativity.
Success hatches your biggest fans,
While Obscurity hosts these same Cynics.
I may have come out the gate last...
But with one fat check:
You're following *My* footsteps.

The scent of cash is strong,
Like a Wolfpack that smells their
Own Blood.
You brought me to this planet,
but my Expression is Agamic.
But Sometimes Expression has Costs
That not even Cash can Change:

It is Family that cuts a Budding Adult,
who would have gladly opened her blouse...
It is Family that changes a lyric —
Reducing A Booming Voice to a squeak of a mouse.

I will not change even one word,
Or a single letter in-between these pages,
You're either with me or you're against me:
A sentiment I'd pass down to generations
For Ages.

CHAPTER 20

HUMBLE PIE

Humble Pie

Is revenge or pussy sweeter?
Why have one when you can
Have Two?
I'd lay my critics to bed,
What can I say I got a
Mean Sweet Tooth.

Third World

White girls might leave me out In the Snow,
&
Black girls might Shut Me Out;

But Latina America opens up

A Tropical Third World.

Affirmative Action

She had only allowed Vanilla
to occupy her mouth,
Wouldn't give change a chance:
Her mind was facing Due South...

FREEDOM!

One taste of Chestnut
is
All it Took —
&
Instantly:
She was Hooked!
Now the bars are Free
to sticks of hard Dark Choc'late,
Her Doors Are Now Open,
But still they Knock It/
Once her surface was Cracked,
There was no going Back/
Now she'll give me a shot,
She boils at the sight of my pot/
The proof is in her choice of pudding,
And Now that this new life is budding...
I can't just keep Relaxin',
I gotta March on Up — Takin' Affirmative Action!

CHAPTER 21

THE ANTIDOTE

I Held a Lorikeet Today

I Held a Lorikeet Today —
Both
Free
to
Hold
Its Wings...
My open palm seizes the moment
This warm season graciously
Brings.
I expected
Another quotidian day,
In a prosaic site tinctured in gray,
When in from the Wind
Flew In —
A Pop Fly
Like a stray Blue Jay.
My hand was as still as the air,
As un-shifting as my beholden stare.

I admiringly hawked at its wings —
Each
Assorted
Prismatic
Shade.
As the sun beamed down on us,
I knew I had it made
In the Shade.
This was a once in a lifetime sight,
And I had the perfect bird's-view.

I captured these six seconds,
And held it for the rest of the day.

My face had a serene tint,
In-Hidden a camouflaged grin...
Although I knew it'd soon fly away...

And I'd sit alone again.

Full Story of Boy Meets Girl

Boy Meets Girl,
Girl is Blasé,
Boy offers Soul,
Girl: "That's Okay."

The Matchmaker of Loneliness

How is it that she can be so Nonchalant —
While I Am so Naïve?
What is to blame for this false hope —
In the face of reality?
What is it that makes her so immune
To this spreading infection that consumes me so?

Is she an un-feeling bitch?
Does she have another?
Is it possible that one can be *born*
So indifferent and blasé?
Has she been ruined for the world by
Its own selfish consumption?
There *must* be a Reason —
For while she is routinely friendly,
I stand with my heart in hand
And my soul left wide open,
While her door gently closes.
Whenever I approach the welcoming breach —
The Bond almost has a physical weight —
As anything tangible would,
Until reality comes crashing down,
As deep down I knew it would.
Oh, what is it that is there —
That only I can't see?
It is the Matchmaker called "Loneliness,"
Who only works for Me.

The Reminder

I saw a pretty girl today,
And she reminded me of You...
Then I saw another —
And to my surprise,
She did too.

I saw a Greyhound,
And all the Passengers,
A Fire Truck,
An Extinguisher...

Lake Michigan,
A folded tent,
A Ferris Wheel,
A small basset...

A bumblebee,
A Tiny Dwarf,
A ladybug,
An infected wart...

A bathroom stall,
A composite sketch,
A sewer rat,
A polished jet...

A Meadowlark,
A Sandy Beach,
A Hornet's Nest,

A Parakeet...

Today I saw a lot of things...
They all reminded me of you.
Then when I saw you —
You reminded me of me.

The Deepest Apology

I know what you're going through.
I know how you feel.
I Would be there for you —
I too feel what you don't feel.
I too yearn to be touched —
Understood.
Loved.
Yes I do know how you feel —
You're not the Only 1.

I feel your S.O.S. —
But I can't be the one to
Save You...
I can't see it,
Find You,
Touch You...
But I can empathize with you.
We are Companions and
Don't Even Know It —
Just because we don't Know Each Other.

We still share an Empty Room,
That makes us mates in Bloom.

I know you're somewhere out there...
And if you are reading these words:
This apology was meant for you,
Though I'm sure they'll go unheard.

The Antidote

I've been Poisoned.

i once had vigor.
life,
salubrity.

now it feels like
any day
could be my last.

i lay in prostration
more'an any inpatient.
life so flat
it feels
i'll flatline
any time.

i'm ailed by a venom,

a toxic
contagion.

please, grace,

retrieve me.

Consulting from Previous Experience

Put Away that Scalpel!
There's been a change of plans!
Take away those tubes!
He's about to stand!
Unplug that EKG —
Stop writing on those sheets!
Turn off all those monitors!
His heart's about to beat!
Reshelf the Defibrillator!
There's no longer any need!
Take off those Masks!
Now we All can breathe!
Throw away them needles!
And Save us All the Sight!
You only need her Smile —
It brought Me back to life.

CHAPTER 22

SOLITARY

The Mugging

Please, direct me to a
Police Station
Where I can report this
Heinous Crime:

I was standing about —
Minding my own business —
And there she was,
All cocky-like...
Smiling, alluring, inviting...
Being the caring, upright citizen that I am:
I befriended her.
I was doing fine on my own!
She came to ME!
For had you seen that smile and felt
That warm glowing vibe,
You would have done the same.
The next thing I know, she's gone...
I'm down, crying for help,

Heartless — Left Broke...
I never saw it coming.
If it's not a crime, then at least it's a sin,
If you can't help me please tell me who can —
Because she's free to strike again.

Cold Case Files

This will surely go down
as one of life's
Great Mysteries.
As hot as our chemistry is,
How can you be so cold?
The fire is blowing right in front of us...
How the hell can you not feel that?
Don't bother letting a small thing called "science"
Apprehend your view of the facts.
You don't need to practice Forensics
To see this crumb of miles...
But just because you're Resisting —
This remains in the
Cold Case Files.

The Biggest Crime

You are a murdering Freak,
&
You're still not doing time...
But for you to have love while we don't —
Is the Biggest Crime.

Solitary

Confinement.
Solitude.
These circumstances I rationalize,
When the facts are much more clear:
I've been Institutionalized.

Like a stubborn inmate,
I refuse to take the blame...
Taking credit for this imprisonment
Would further tarnish my name.
No, it wasn't me!
I was set up from the Go...
The world conspired against me —
I reached out, and they said, "No."
I justify my sentence —
With each stamped letter
&
Eloquent Sentence...
I point out and not to the sky,
Chains Locked on my Repentance.
Though I make a good case,
The Evidence is right in my face:
I don't want out of this place.

When a man is thrown in solitary,
He won't come out the same...
The longer he is boxed in —
The less of him remains.

Not even in General Population —
I'm in this small black hole...
Soft hands tried to pull me out —
And I dismissed my chance at parole.

Most prisoners take what they can get,
A Halfway-House would Suffice...
If I should leave this hole —
I want a Paradise.

What's more frightening than living in a hole?
Making the hole your home.

I've come to expect this slop —
That you're so kind to serve...
But I don't want sloppy seconds,
So I'll keep that seat reserved.
I've had my chances to flea,
With a decree of "Not Guilty,"
When I saw what arms awaited...
I had to Change my Plea.
So I am just a fraud,
I've Chose to serve this time...
I may be physically confined —
But not even I can shackle my mind.

CHAPTER 23

I WISH I COULD DANCE LIKE MICHAEL JACKSON

The Unbuildable Wall

For there are Boundaries —
Much Wider Than Any City Limit.
Property Lines that bid no X.
With owners and Jurisdiction
too ubiquitous to Lease.
Trespassers Heed the Warnings,
Return to Permitted Provinces
within a comfort zone
with walls that easily contain the blaring sounds
that wake neighbors
and is heard miles away.
Yet there are some sounds
that no wall can contain.
Clapton's Chords Changed the World,
NWA's Expression Transmitted far beyond
The Streets of Compton,
Fleetwood Macked Over Gender Lines,
And Sarah's Angelic Voice...
Should be Remembered by *All*.

So When Tyrone Jackson
Blasts Madonna for the world to hear —
Remember:

Greatness Knows No Boundaries

Ego

Put down your macho ego,
It's ok to love
Beyoncé's "Ego."
It's ok to bow to Queens,
That doesn't make you a parasite,
And not the least bit "queer,"
Turn it up louder — it's alright.
You don't have to like Bette Midler
From a Distance.
You're so far away…
Doesn't anybody just love pure art, anymore?
Carole was a Queen among "Kings,"
Don't subject royalty to your demean.

It's ok to love Beyoncé's "Ego,"
and not just for Kanye's Propane Spit…
It could very well be her best,
Even though not on her
"Greatest Hits."
It's ok to sit and look,
but Stop hiding behind their looks.
Admit it, you like her voice,
Not just because "she's hot,"
Being macho is OK,
But stop trying to be something you're not.
That Glitz, Those Steps, Those Moves —
All dazzling in that video:
Created a Universal Gem —
Made in an epicene studio.

Her creativity spread all over that piano,
Ohhh and the way she sang in the end...
Could bring any man to tears —
It was truly as beautiful as her glow...

Please, put down your Macho Ego,
You can love Beyoncé's "Ego."

I Wish I Could Dance Like Michael Jackson

If living a life full of
Isolation & Loneliness,
devoid of genuine companionship
or a Soulmate
Meant having my soul's remains splattered all over
500 Million others'...
That is a trade
I'd gladly Make.

For that would Make me 499,999,999 times Richer
Than the most fortunate of men.

If I could get through an endless
string of nights of
being a misunderstood misfit
In return for drowning in something deeper
than all the hate in the world
Until something is conceived that is loved
By a surrogate family of every race...
My choice would be
Black & White.

To be an outcast in my own nation
and seek refuge in a foreign land
would be just splendiferous,
If I could throw a going away party
and have the whole world as my dance partner

For just one measly 30-year dance.

And even better
if long after I've exited —
My party continues to spin
for partygoers to tuck their heads down
with a hand placed gently atop
with high twist-kicks until a new generation
comes in to pick up the love.

The tears of a Child
and anguish of a Man
would be comforted by
a sympathetic audience
Beholding the thrilling transformation
of pain into art:
Within every single note, chord, and hard-bitten
expression.
It is no wonder why so many tears
Could be found in audiences,
for the pain would physically jump out of my body
and splash into my sea of brethren.
If funerals could have live performances of the
departed
With no eulogies spoken —
Only the raw expression of the deceased found
In his Voice
&
In his Dance:
It would only equal the Power
of
Just Another of his Performances.

Those would be my greatest moves —
With my blood left on the Dance Floor.
To feel the embrace of the remaining
Unconditional Family
Who have Seen the
Bad,
Heard the Worse,
And Read the Worst...
Nothing could Beat It.
If so many millions could share that pain,
Then how many millions share this wish?

I Wish I Could Dance Like Michael Jackson,
But if I could...
Michael Jackson wouldn't be Michael Jackson —
We All Would.

For All the Unwritten Songs

Sam's Masterpieces
Would take the average artist
Many Sleepless Nights...
For him it came so easy —
Just Another Saturday Night.
Each song went beyond the lyrics —
It bared his soulful spirit.
Each year a new hit hit —
No sign that he would quit.
But he left before giving us more —
Departed right before thirty-four.

When he went the Change had Come,
For all Successors to Use It...
The final Chain from his Gang —
Was "Sweet Soul Music."
Jimi had just begun his shift,
Before he played his last riff...
Now they're both playing the "Night Shift,"
With great backup they are with.

Karen Carpenter,
Marvin Gaye...
Weren't done but that's okay...
I believe like the Commodores:
That the dead continue to play.

Elvis Presley,
John Lennon —

Played Guitars that had them Crowned in advance…
They may be resting in peace,
But their Piece won't give
Peace a Chance.

This is for the great that died young,
For all the songs that were never sung,
& If I should prematurely plunge:

Don't question if another line was in me,
You can bet your ass that I had plenty.

CHAPTER 24

A CAUSE FOR CELEBRATION

Blow the Whistle

Leave me out coach.
I am no good to you broken.
I am in no shape — mental or emotional —
To be put in without soon chokin'.
For what is a high compliment for most,
Is bittersweet to me...
They say that I am young,
But my life feels 63.
Right as I am prepared —
To throw in this bloody towel,
You keep putting me back in —
And I keep crying foul.
What will it take for you to see
That I just cannot score?
I appreciate these many opportunities,
but they keep slamming me to the floor.
It is flagrant and offensive.
Tell me —
Where is the flag?!

They travel over me so much
The Whole World must have jet lag.
I do not belong in this game,
No matter how many chances I have,
A scrub is still a scrub,
Please let me sit this second half.
I hope the gray and wrinkles hurry,
And my hair will symbolize my loss...
I am getting tired of ejecting myself,
Before I have a chance to get tossed.
Take my word for it, coach —
I am getting too old for this game...
I know you don't see it that way —
Just because I look the same.

Fair Game

If it's charm you seek,
He's got plenty to go around,
He's the type to move along,
While you want another round.
He's got the lines to bend 'em,
And young hearts — he breaks 'em,
See, he doesn't call it "keeps,"
He only plays "make 'em take 'em."
When it comes to confidence,
He's sure he won't disappoint...
His wit is razor sharp —
Or a knife tip — ah, you get the point.
His tongue has a way with words
That I cannot help but envy...
I try to express like he does —
But the words stay trapped within' me.
He's got that thing called "Game,"
And the ladies he sure does play 'em...
While he easily closes the deal,
They actually expect me to pay 'em.

Now as he plays the field,
I'm still here tryin' to court 'em.

If there were a neutral ground
With rules where I could win...
I'd produce like any player,
and score again and again.
This turf belongs to him,

The outcomes remain the same...
But If I had a say in the rules,
Then You would be Fair Game.

He may have what I don't have,
But it is only on the surface...
If we could play on my terms,
His charm would serve no purpose.
As I look into your eyes,
If only you could know what I think...
Your mind would freeze in time,
Even your lids would forget to blink.
That is all that it would take:
You seeing how I see you...
You'd see me as I am,
Not that hoax you can't see through.
For with words he has the edge,
& he can charm you out your pants...
But if you could read my thoughts,
He wouldn't stand a chance.

The Prospect

It's easy for you to
Sit this one out,
Your number
Is Always Called...
I know you hear many offers —
Now I'd like to make My pitch:

They won't allow me to pay you,
They say that's against the rules...
I can only offer my heart —
OOOOO
If you play, I'll take you to School!

Fences

I could've always scored,
If I hadn't left my guard up…
I stayed watching in the backcourt,
When I could've had a lay-up.

I hardly threw a pitch —
How could I expect to catch her?

My gates wouldn't let them pass,
I turned the masses to "denses…"
Just throw one more curve my way…
&
I swear — I'll Swing for the Fences.

A Cause for Celebration

There are good days.

Days to Celebrate, in fact.

I can still recall the 49ers routing the
Denver Broncos in '89,
Brock Lesnar winning the UFC Heavyweight
Championship,
And every single victory of the 2009 Minnesota
Vikings.
A fleeting joy in honor of men I do not know —
Will not know...
Men who are a point of envy for many —
Today, for me, are a
Cause for Celebration.

A sense of emptiness abiding inside
weighing in heavier than any
Combatant
Is knocked down to size by a giant figure
Larger than Life enough to stand up to this
Arrogant Bully.
For in this moment, my happiness is no less
Than the most content man in the bar.
It is a moment to cherish. A *night* to cherish.
For as early as 'morrow, the bully reemerges

* * *

My hero has been sent fishing,
With the others still at bay...
But on this June Afternoon,
The Bully has been shoved away.
With a roster of 7 Billion,
Heroes are always among us,
Sometimes it is easy to forget:

Players don't always have a Jersey.

If not one, then how many happy faces equate to
The Big One?
With millions lonely, starving, homeless, broke, sick, dying...
The odds are Undisputed:
There are also millions happy, content, & loved or once loved.

How many alpha males need to bang the unapproachable?
How many girls does the undergrad have to run through a semester?
How many times does mind-blowing, earth shattering sex need to take place
Between strangers, lovers, or spouses?
How many first loves must be spawned?
How many babies must be born into the happy homes
Of Families built on true love?
How many high school sweethearts need to evolve into
College — and finally — matrimonial lovers?

A CAUSE FOR CELEBRATION

How many underdogs have to win the girl?
How many special, rare women of dreams need to be won?
How many DREAMS need to be won?
How many people need to want absolutely nothing more out of life?
How many equates to one championship?
Please, pick a number, and I can guarantee
That it will be met.

These victories of men no less familiar than the greatest championship ball player
Are feats equally as unattainable for the lonely.
What comes naturally to some is awe-inspiring for others.
That girl, that happiness, that family, is as difficult and unimaginable for some
As holding up Lombardi itself.
So it is from the stands that I offer this round of applause,
With cheers for those carrying out breathtaking performances —
For the worthy and noble who found their life partner:
Enjoy that Champagne.
Because Every Single Day:
Another Hero Wins a Ring.

It is A Cause for Celebration —
I am Truly Happy for You...
Now if I could just keep this feeling,
Then that would Make Two.

CHAPTER 25

BREAKING LOVE

LoL....What Happened?

I thought your love was eternal?
I thought your love nest would become paternal —
With a future home filled with little runts?
I guess the time span of "forever..."
Is about Eight Months.

Union of Funds

Let us join this once happy couple
In a life of Acrimony...
They wanted to build a life,
Now they only want Alimony.

Breaking Love

"Love Can Move Mountains,"
While still
"Standing the Test of Time..."
In spite of wisdom's common tokens,
Love is quite Easily Broken.

Romance's Greatest Poet,
Love's Greatest Romance,
A Poet's Greatest Lover:
Are all exposed to the advance
of Flesh.

The Fragrance of Love
Is Not
As Potent as Lust,
This Natural Truth
Is what All Couples can Trust.

It seems their slumbering scene,
Put all suspicions to rest...
Though all this really means:
They're not yet put to the test.

Even if conscience and
Fraud Records are Clear,
This is only until —
Temptation's Head Appears.

Frequent requests

From a potential mistress,
Many men could resist,
Now try a Worldly Goddess.

That gleam in her eye
Is only shining for one,
Yet that scream of a sigh
Could be evoked by a ton.

It's not a question of love,
Or a matter of Faith...
What determines your fates —
Is lurking predator traits.

The most devoted spouse
Can still be aroused
By a face in the crowd
If situation allowed.

Some girls may be Chaste,
And some guys may be Saints,
But one Room for Mistakes
Is really All that It Takes.

The lights go out,
Upstairs rendered dim...
All Digital Control —
Handed over to Him.

Cupid's Savory Potion,
Is what open mouths show,

BREAKING LOVE

But in this unlit Heaven —
Their sweeter juices flow.

This carnal paradise —
No mind could forget,
These illicit memories —
Do not reject regret.

The frame, pillar and post
Crack during this primitive poke,
Vows gone cold without cover —
Merge with all the articles Broke.

To "Break Love" is drenched
In Lust,
It's a term for
Rebels of Passion...
It upholds that
For a Positive Action —
Lies a Stimulating
Wicked Reaction.

While Couples deny this Test,
so they can continue to be Making Love...
Lovers aren't just Making Lust,
They're also "Breaking Love."

CHAPTER 26
CHURCH OF LOVE

Savior

It's been too many days
Since I have laughed all day...
There's been too few girls
Who've made me feel this way.
Some girls reach out to Bad Boys,
And eventually get dismissed...
If you're looking for a soul to save,
It doesn't get Much Worse than this.
Every girl wants to be the only one —
Who can turn a man around...
Well now is your big chance,
Only you make me walk this cloud.
I can't just open up freely,
I know that most guys can...
But once you walk away,
I may never feel this way again.
You might be the only girl for me,
How hilarious is that?
Yet the more I sit and think about it —
It's actually quite sad.
I just know I needed this smile,
& It must be thanks to you...
Because it had been a while.

Every Girl wants a Love Story,
With Triumph against All Odds...
To be my Only Savior —
Is an ending written by the Hands of God.

Pure

Pure.
Untouched.
Unadulterated.

Pure.
Spotless.
Stainless.

Pure.
Defeating a Crowded Room.
Willed by a Larger Force.

Pure.
Not for the Physical,
Not for the Sex.

Pure.
Oxygen.
Crystalline.

Pure.
Achromatic.
Purged.

Pure.
Not for the humor.
Not for your entertainment.

Pure.
Who I Am.
What I Am.

Pure.
Halcyon.
Fetal Snow.

Pure.
Only
You
&
Only
Me.

Pure.
No Pasts.
Right Now.

Pure.
Only this moment
&
Our unblemished future.

Pure.
Untarnished.
Unbroken.

Pure.
No one before.
No one after.

Pure.
Uncontaminated.
Unplowed.

Pure.
Unattainable.
Unreachable.

Pure.
Pure Imagination.
Pure Fiction.

Not even
Pure Luck.

Reserved for
Lucid Dreams
&
Heaven...

With Angels
Sheathed in White.

Pure.

Church of Love

You know I worship you.
You are Everything
and Everywhere.
I may not always want to believe in you,
But I need to.
I need you.

I Need You

To

Deliver me to Temptations,
Be my Saving Grace...
Show me a Spiritual Harlot,
With an Angel's Face.
Compassionately take me in,
Absolve me of my Sins...
of not indulging sooner —
Condemned to failing Lent.
Hollowed is thy hall,
I was born with many flaws,
Baptize me in these walls,
Save me as you did Saul.
I need some heavenly hugs,
from a loving Trinity:
The Mother, then the Daughter,
&
The Blazed Step Child "Serenity."
This isn't a mockery of piety,

Or a heathen's attempt to Blaspheme,
These are my actual prayers,
Yet your presence remains unseen.
Still I keep the Faith,
When non-believers say you're not real...
It's my only hope at a Miracle,
So still I bow and kneel.

Hands clamped — as tight as a
Nun's Uterus,
This
Out of Body Birth
Was Delivered by
Mary's Fetus.

My eyes await a glimpse,
but This Sign you don't Exist —
Augers an
Inner Apocalypse.

I close my eyes again...
I walk into
The Darkness...
Hell's Gate Awaits,
But I've already seen
The Abyss.

Eyes Closed, Hands Clamped, Knees Sore,
This miracle I can't perform alone,
So the Choir Takes the Floor.

My eyes Closed
&
Their Mouths Agape,
They harmonized every pitch —
No-Note chimed in late.
It wasn't lyrics and notes,
Just a low "hmm" mixed with the sound of "Ha"
Up and Up it Went —
With the love of my beloved Ma.
Each face of this righteous choir
Went Unchanged,
Unaltered,
Unmoved,
As they carried this disciplined stillness —
My soul moved through the room.

As their voices spread through my temple,
My soul pervaded this Temple.
Through the Rows Pew by Pew —
Un-Bared Crosses it now leapt through…
I felt a new chapter at the alter,
My vow of faith I aimed to renew.
Past the Tabernacle off the Stained Glass —
That's when the light went in me,
Nearly blind but again I can see.

If I had more energy, I would have danced…
I would have thrown my arms up,
Chanting, "Hallelujah!"

But the energy I had was so overpowering...that
I could only offer my head to the lead singer's
bosom....
For once she moved.
She took me into her arms, as the choir ceased to
sing.

Now We Pray.

Love,

Though this doctrine I often question, I let doubters
shroud the answers. You Are Out There Somewhere:
I can't let non-believers steal my hope. I will wait. I
believe. I am willing to wait.....

Forever and Ever,

Amen.

I will Believe what I choose to Believe —
They cannot rob me or break the Eighth...
I'm still awaiting the First-Coming,
So I have to Keep the Faith.

CHAPTER 27

ENVYING THE BLIND

Envying the Blind

I am blessed to own All my
Senses; Still
one feels more like a curse...
They
Recoup and help me Regroup.
Heal so I can Deal.
While four help me live,
One pushes me over the edge.

Mosquitoes bestir a Twitch,
Unwavering Bites
Leave
An Itch...
Pustules and Bumps you'll carry,
But skin patches without
A Stitch.
A threatened skunk sprays,
The stench lasts days —

Sometimes even weeks...
Though the smell will certainly reek:
Breaths will outlast it.
The neighbor's collie barks all night —
Warding off your rest,
But it's only a matter of time —
Till the Problem is Put to Sleep.

Beef cuts Please the Taste,
Particularly the Leanest...
But your tongue will
Have a Cow —
When it's Revealed
You're sucking the
Penis.

There's one sense that Cannot heal —
It only gets worse with time.

Bad food you chew and spit out,
Are more selective when you
Decide to Eat Out,
I've sniffed and listened for a treatment,
But I See that there's no way out.
Gorgeous Women
I am Forced to See,
I can Look but I cannot find —
One that will walk with me,
That's why I Envy the Blind.

ENVYING THE BLIND

Being blind has its pitfalls,
But to all the blind I say:
Hey! You! Look Up!
There's an Upside to being Blind.

Breaking Even with the Poor

Famine.
Starvation.
Destitution.
Richly Impoverished.
Barely clothed.
Unfed Mouths.
Monotonous Tears
And
Sinking Fears.
Shacks in Outbacks.
Cold Alleys.
Barren Souls.

My sincere sympathy you have...
Spare Change
You will surely Own...
Not out of any debt,
Those in poverty I do not owe.
There's one thing you have that I don't:
At least you are sheltered in Love.
We exchange Hungers and both haven't Eaten,
The way I see it —
That makes us Even.

CHAPTER 28

TRAVEL ARRANGEMENTS

Travel Arrangements

Like a drifter I travel light,
My feet move quick that's a
Natural Habit —
That could help explain —
The reason why I don't like baggage.

I'd gladly take your load off,
But I can't accept his load…
I can't clean up your past issues,
I'm afraid I have my own.
I turned some away at the gate,
Because their luggage weighed too heavy…
I chose to fly solo,
With a weight only I could carry.
I'd be willing to make arrangements,
I could deal with another man's semen…
I'll take in your baggage,
If you'll accept my demons.

The Proposal

Hello, Beautiful...

W-wait where you going?!
Look, usually I don't do this, but...
Babe, you got my blood flowin'!
Admit it, we've had fun, my sweet.
Let's make it last more than a week.
Listen, I've tried to accept my past life...
Hell, I've tried with all my might,
But I can tell by the
Big Fights
&
Bright Lights...
That Good Golly — You Alright!
Some think you're too fast...
But you are just my speed...
The casinos and those fine hotels —
Was all the proof I need!
And we haven't even scratched the surface yet...
Imagine:
Strippers, Hookers, Shows...
And let us not forget:
All the tourist Hoes!
Hell, we've already seen the Buffets,
That action speaks for itself...
Too Much is Never Enough —
This gluttony can't be bad for my health!
So what do you say, huh?

Will you have me,
baby?
Wait, sweetheart, why you laughin'?
There's a Chapel! We can make this happen!

You're My Wilson

I've Cast Away my doubts!
I'm sure of these powerful feelings!
I wouldn't sit and wait for most,
But for You I'm more than willing!
See, I'm stuck here on this Island...
And you're all the Companionship
I Got....
Yeah I know you barely know me,
But why don't you give me a shot?
Ok, I know I might sound crazy,
Maybe I should start to explain...

See, when you're as lonely as I am,
Your sanity is in constant danger...
I've tried to swim offshore,
but the impending outcome
Was no Cliffhanger.
See, it's like that Tom Hanks movie...
I can't remember the title...
He even named a Volleyball,
Something so absurd was suddenly vital.
I don't recall its name either —
But I'm sure you get the point...
You're my only outside interaction,
If you retreat I'll snap
joint by joint.
No, don't be afraid!
I'm talking about my sanity!
So don't leave your fellow man stranded!

Show a little humanity!
I may be stuck on this Island,
But you lift me Higher than Jackie Wilson!
Oh! I Remember Now!
Yeah! You're My Wilson!

Rock Stars

I want to fly away.
Far, Far Away.
I want to Rocket
To the Moon,
And not return
For a "Long, Long Time."

There's too much pressure in here,
Even with this balanced Ozone,
They say Mercury has no Atmosphere,
So I'd feel right at Home.
Maybe one Drop of Jupiter
Is all it takes to find my Angel,
We'd fly to Saturn and exchange Rings,
In Space-time where we won't "Miss a Thing."
I may be dreaming too much,
My mind has already seen Mars…
I want to go even further —
Far Past all Orbs & Stars.
Maybe if I conquer a Venus —
Then I could see Uranus!
I'd Rock Stars like the Neptunes
& Make a Home right on the Moon.
They say planets can't support life,
That
Only One is to Human Worth…
But I know otherwise:
It's far too cold on Earth.

CHAPTER 29

WRITER WITHOUT A CAUSE

Stop, Type, and Roll

Can't Sit Still,
Thoughts in constant motion...
Being too modest would
Make me a Liar:
The reason I'm on this roll —
Is due to me being on fire.

Art Kingdom: Do as I say and Not as I Do

This is My Royal Palace!
I condemn thee who steal my workload!
Thou shalt not steal one's art!
But sorry, Prince, I'mma Still Download…

Maybe I Should Stay In Tonight

Maybe I should stay in tonight,
My thoughts may not be safe…
I couldn't live with myself if I died —
And all this work went out to waste.
I know it's Saturday Night,
But this book is almost through…
Just because I'm living now —
Doesn't mean I'm Bullet Proof.
Thug, if you *must* Drive-By,
And fill me up with lead,
Can you wait just a wee bit longer?
When I'm done, I won't care if I'm dead.

Blood, Sweat & Tears

If this work could make me bleed —
I'd bleed
Profusely.
If typing worked up a sweat —
I'd sweat like a pet
at the sight
of a Net.
Just take my words for it,
I'm grateful for all of your ears…
I can't give you Blood and Sweat,
So I hope you'll settle for Tears.

Just One Minute!

Love! Hold On! I'm almost done!
Let me just finish this work,
And Then I'll have fun!
Time is running out!
Soon love will come out!
I gotta hurry up now,
And put this book out!
Cuz Once I have you,
I'll have no more time!
So I must hurry fast,
And finish these lines!

2 Minutes

I wrote this one within 2 minutes,
Just gimme one sec
And I'll be finished,
I'm breakin' down walls
Like Cathy Dennis —
Fastest Poem Ever
I'm in the
World of Guinness.

Writer without a Cause

My birthright name is Clyde Aidoo,
If you don't like me
Then Hell,
Fuck You....

* * *

I don't write for you,
I only write for me...
Not tryna change the World,
I just want it on the streets!

Press Releases,
Reek like Feces,
My prose so tight
It shattered out in Pieces!!!

Yankee-Dooda-Doo
I don't rock Cowboy Boots,
I like walking shoes —
My feet are blacker than Roots!!!!!

De's shoes—you couldn't walk a mile —
People think they know me
All I do is smile!!

I'm Free-Free at Last —
Them chains a thing of the past,
Cuz

Ulysses S. Grant
Whooped
Robert Lee's ASS!!!!!!!!!!!!!

This hate — I can't understand,
but
the Time you're Wastin'
makes You a Fan!

Now I'm here, but wasn't sure I'd Make It,
Wasn't granted reparations
So I Had to *Take* it!!!!!

And now I'm throwin'-a-Party,
& I hope you'll join me —
Now I'm livin' "Hardee"
And eaten out at "Show-Me's."

Scantily Clad Ass —
You know I gotta look,
I like livin' fast
so I can put it in the Books!!!!

Knee High—no more than age of Five —
I put pen to pad —
Most fun I'd ever Had!

Grew up and I was writin' 'bout nothin':
Sports, Games, Wrestlin'
New words I stayed steady huntin'!

Shipped out to the back of the woods —
No one ever saw me
cuz I moved out the hood!

Suburbia Found and Basement Bound,
I knew I had to write —
I couldn't shake a Noun!

All day I thought of something new,
Started IWF
Then fronted 2-K-W!!
That's a brand, you wouldn't understand —
It's only for my partners
Who helped
Build
Me a
Stand!!

Fist of Rage — I could never be,
I leave the anger to the B
Or should I say, "Cody?"
Search for meaning — don't even bother,
This is inside:
They were the sons to my father!!

Who knew that after six long years
We'd put in print our work
from being buried in dirt?
Spelling errors,
Jacked up grammar,
Self-Published, Team-Made,

Fulfilled without being Paid!

Year later I branched out my passion,
Went out on my Own, then:
"This is Pro Wrestlin'!"

Slightly-Vindicated this-time I had-a-firm-grade-it
They put it out for me
Was proud but was never jaded...

Though this step was through
Still had some work to do
'Til I could hit real stands
and bring it out to You!!!

Steal my thoughts —
I'm callin' me a lawyer,
It took some time:
But now I Got One 4 Ya!!!!

Erik Phelps — he knows the CD,
Back when I was boxed in
He was the only one who knew me!!
Kid Rocked it —
Was the Devil Wit'out Cause —
The CD shaped me — I gave a round of applause!!!

I might not be the best,
Or even the realest,
But somewhere-out-there:
I Know Somebody's Gotta Feel This!!!!!

If they don't
then well, Fuck Off —
I'll just keep moving on
and they'll ask — "Where You At?"

Obscurity I know,
Know it all to well,
But it's a new day now:
I cannot help but excel!

Kid Rock: He "Babe Ruthed" a Platinum —
He broke his way through,
"Wasting Time" was my Anthem!

And If I fail,
I'll keep on and try,
I'll keep on writing words
&
Only God Knows Why!!!!

Prevail I must,
In my skills I trust,
Was muggy for a minute
Now leavin' doubts in the dust!

I guarantee success,
As the jaws hit the floors:

Aidoo — Art of Mind:

I'M HITTIN' BOOKSTORES!!!!!!!!!!!!!!!!!!!!!!!!!!!!

CHAPTER 30

THE GREATEST ART OF ALL

Headphones

I wish I could borrow
Your Headphones,
And I'd gladly lend you mine.
More than anything in this world —
I wish I could lend you mine.

If I could channel each wave,
Each moment that sensation hits,
I'd gladly Unchain every Melody.

It's not enough to share the same playlist,
I want you to feel every
Creative
Inspiring
Invigorating
Life-Reflecting
Note that surfs my body.

Oh, I want to share yours, too.

I know, so tragically I can't.
Maybe someday I can,
Keep bobbin' ya head for me, till then.

If we could just borrow one another's
Headphones:

This World would be in Perfect Harmony.

Not Sorry to Disappoint

What were you expecting? Fucking Shakespeare?
Love poems are a big hit,
Now ask me if I care.
You were expecting to shed some tears?
Only to see mine flow instead...
Well I ain't Maya Angelou,
Or that other crap you've read.
If you were expecting Love Poems I feel bad for you,
son...
Got Over 99 Poems
But
My Bliss Ain't 1.

O.C.A.

I grew up in an urbanized town.
Couldn't complain.
I was surrounded by
Family, Friends, a Family-Friendly School…
On the outside lived guns & violence,
But during the day
I could roam free and play.
My childhood was filled with laughter,
I was rarely ever alone.
Relocated to a safer outside environment
In a trade-off for inner violence.
The house suddenly got empty,
And
The new school was more like a prison.
I was fresh meat and they were
Hungry Inmates.
My body remained intact.
Even my mind.
It's my spirit and trust
They raped.

So the basement was my refuge.
I went off to college so I could Feel Good…
Still, I remained out of touch.
I had a propensity to lose
while the rest of the world seemed to gain,
There's one thing I have that they don't:
No One has My Name.

With the Basement as my institution,
I Committed myself to Art —
Until death does us part.

No, it's not easy
When
Everyone else is different
From You,
But I'm proud I'm my own kind:
There's only One Clyde Aidoo.

The Greatest Art of All

Tonight, it's Friday Night.
6/25, 26:00.
Tonight, like many other nights,
Was as anti-climatic as an old wives' tale.
Yet it's a tale I must tell —
For there's a larger tale,
Nonetheless…

A tale that speaks to us all:
From your ear's eyes
To my finger's lips:

I chopped my lumbered visage,
To re-introduce the landscape underneath…
After-shaved after I bathed,
And Then
The real show showed.

The mirror was the screen,
And it featured a one man act.
By the time tonight's wardrobe
was complete,
If these walls could speak,
They'd wish Da Champ
God Speed.

Even the toilet —
With all it's gone through
And what's went through —

THE GREATEST ART OF ALL

It is this night that it would speak.
It'd echo the wall's sentiments
and be the applause of
Ladies & Gentlemen.

No one saw the first act...
That's quite alright.
The second act is when
The Real Show Begins Anyway.

Swag was my middle name,
You can't sell this and I can't
Take it Back...
An opinion would be in my own head —
The mirror Proved it Fact.
My style is just Too Phat...
Can Someone call 911!?
My Swag just had a
Heart-Attack!!

What's existed will exist forever:
Forever in these minutes.
Tonight, like so many nights before:
Success nor Embrace do not shape
Reflections of Time.

The club was completely dead.
The Rock Star made a quiet Cameo.
No autographs, pics, or screaming —
Only groups, friends, and
Silent Indifference.

No, no...not the first time.
Certainly not the last.

Went back home the same as I went out.
I could have
Pick-pocketed, stole or robbed
Without a soul who could Identify Me.
The crowd was as dead as the venue,
But the Rock Star Still Came Through.

Witnesses help validate,
Which is why we share our ideas...
But our ideas are still our ideas —
Even when they fall on deaf ears.

I neglected to change on return,
No, this is my outfit for the night...
If it's an Image you need to picture —
I Precisely Wear Black and White.

Thinking back to all the other times —
I didn't even have *these* words to report.
Just me & night's dark, dark secret...
As concealed as some of the greatest of thoughts —
From poets you've never Heard of —
Let alone Read,
Singers you've never Heard —
Let alone Read about...

People.

THE GREATEST ART OF ALL

People you've never Seen.
Heard of.
Read about:
With ideas.
Jokes.
Concepts.
Love.
That you couldn't fathom to exist.
Please, get over yourself,
In order to *celebrate* yourself...
For it is still Art.
As much as the Mona Lisa
&
The 16th Chapel.
Ah, but of course you know those...
It is also as much art as
The Art
of Lynn Armstrong's
"Paqui"
And Ricki Losee's
"Winter Refuge."
It is the Art of the most
Pulchritudinous Painting,
The Most
Exquisite Sun
And
Ethereal Breath.
It is the art that you breathe
from Your lungs...

You are not my oxygen

Nor
Am I Yours.

You can talk on the phone for hours,
Even set a record — making it days...
Your every thought cannot be conveyed.

This is not a cause to mourn...
A thought may never leave your body,
That doesn't mean it was never Born.

Your every idea someone else has thought,
But no one else has thought your thoughts:
It's a piece of the highest Auction —
Don't fret because It Can't be Bought.

I wish we could snap this moment,
And attend this exhibit together...
Even if no eyes capture this sight,
"A thing of beauty is a Joy Forever."

These words are without light,
Yet the words on this screen
are my perfect accessory.
My shirt as black as these words,
My pants as white as the page...
My bracelet even blends these colors —
It's a beauty only I will gage.

You won't see any tears from me,
For I'll cherish this memory.

THE GREATEST ART OF ALL

I won't be running down the street,
With the desperation of a
Starving Artist's Plea...
If you have the time — Take Me In...
If not, just leave me be.

This Art will Last Forever.

If there were headstones for all ideas passed,
That wouldn't tell their full stories...
Not any more or less
Than a tomb tells a Legend's
Full Glory.

Your complete love doesn't belong to
Your Spouse.
Your ideas not to
Your Boss.
Your thoughts not to your
Friends,
Boyfriends
Or
Girlfriends....
Not even the best of Soulmates.
For words have
White Gates
That can only allow
So many through.
Their owners aren't the world:
They only belong to you.

George and Whitney once told
Of the Greatest Love of All:
Loving Yourself First
Above All Others…
The same holds true for Art.

Only One Artist
Can vision the film
Before the
World's Premiere.
Only one artist is allowed
To hear
The notes
before The new song drops.
You may think you've heard their best,
After it's left their tongues,
But a singer's greatest composition —
May have never been sung.

These words can be rearranged,
Until perfection sheens…
I'm shining it for the world,
But only I may know what I mean.

The most ambitious Hunter
Survey's
Limited Forests.
The fleetest of Nightingales
Return to their
Respective Nests.
Yards may contain Hunter's Feet,

THE GREATEST ART OF ALL

Land hosts Finite Nests,
but The mind is a boundless
Jungle:
Space-less Thoughts
Are free to trek.

Nothing remains in pure form,
These words I'll surely edit...
But the night of 6/25:
I'm sure I'll never Forget It.

Embrace the genius of others,

But Remember —

Art Lives Inside *You*.

* * *

I think I'll change now.

THE END :'/

Images

Palms and Semi by Donna Marsh .... Pg. vi

Fierce Guardian by Judy Gilbert... Pg. vii

Over by Chet Davis.. Pg. x

Blues Queen by John Penney .... Pg. xi

Reflecting Pool by Chet Davis..Pg. xiv

Artist's Dilemma by Chet Davis..Pg. xv

You Complicated Soul by Juliette Caron..Pg. xviii

Vivid Dreams by Juliette Caron.. Pg. xix

Trash Day by Debi Watson...Pg. xxii

Passing By by Debi Watson..Pg. xxiii

Flower Dance Dark Room by Daniel Colvin...Pg. xxvi

The Entrance Sand Bar — NSW by Joe Cartwright..Pg. xxvii

Long Hair and Innocence by Debi Watson...Pg. xxx

Castle Doorway by Joe Cartwright..Pg. xxxi

Sophia by Daniel Colvin..Pg. 9

Tattoo Bride by Lori Pratico...Pg. 85

Concert by Kari Tirrell...Pg. 165

Each of the above images was granted with the full written consent and permission of the artists. All rights of the images belong to the painter of each respective image.

Special thanks to all of the talented artists who contributed their talents to this book & all of the artists who gave me my headphones.

www.ingramcontent.com/pod-product-compliance
Lightning Source LLC
Chambersburg PA
CBHW071450040426

42444CB00008B/1276